MY SIXTIES

poems by

PJ Krass

Finishing Line Press
Georgetown, Kentucky

MY SIXTIES

Copyright © 2022 by PJ Krass
ISBN 978-1-64662-882-7 First Edition
All rights reserved under International and Pan-American Copyright Conventions. No part of this book may be reproduced in any manner whatsoever without written permission from the publisher, except in the case of brief quotations embodied in critical articles and reviews.

ACKNOWLEDGMENTS

Thank you to the following journals, which originally published these poems, sometimes in earlier versions:

Adirondack Review, "Fatherhood"
Atlanta Review, "Outsourcing My Grief"
Caesura, "Old Dog"
Cathexis Northwest Press, "The Weather Man"
Chaleur, "Sawdust"
Rattle, "All Dressed in Green"
Stickman Review, "Boardwalk Blues"

Deep thanks also to my teachers, colleagues and students at The Writers Studio.

Publisher: Leah Huete de Maines
Editor: Christen Kincaid
Cover Art: David Dew Bruner
Author Photo: Cecilia Lehar
Cover Design: Elizabeth Maines McCleavy

Order online: www.finishinglinepress.com
Also available on amazon.com

Author inquiries and mail orders:
Finishing Line Press
PO Box 1626
Georgetown, Kentucky 40324
USA

Table of Contents

I

My Sixties ... 2

Sawdust ... 4

Code Name Sandalwood ... 5

Beatles vs. Stones ... 6

Personality Posters ... 7

Motown Moves ... 8

Suzy Creamcheese ... 10

Hitchhiking for Beginners ... 11

Wouldn't Have No Luck at All ... 13

Greetings from Asbury Park ... 14

II

Dialing the Muse ... 16

All Dressed in Green ... 17

To Unquenchable Ambition ... 18

Late Bloomer ... 20

Boardwalk Blues ... 21

Crass Beauty ... 22

Hoboken ... 24

Fatherhood ... 25

Outsourcing My Grief ... 26

The Weather Man ... 28

Old Dog ... 29

My Sixties ... 30

For Susan, of course

I

You aren't serious at seventeen.
—Rimbaud

My Sixties

In my little town, the sixties didn't arrive
until the seventies. Elsewhere
the summer of love was greening.
Here, summer was humid and hateful,
a boring blaze of claustrophobia,
its soundtrack the chirruping
of a thousand lovesick frogs.

Woodstock, Chicago and Vietnam
were far away. Here,
woodchucks outnumbered books
by Ginsberg and Brautigan,
and a protest march was harder to find
than the pale possum shot dead
by the speeding crossfire of headlights.
In our town so small, the mailman grinned,
I have a letter from your girlfriend,
and it was true, even if she wasn't.

Nights, the hollers of short-fused fathers
rumbled across the hollows of cul-de-sacs.
Days, my friends and I flew to ragged fields
of overgrown farms, sold to developers,
but not developed yet, fallow
as an aimless Sunday.
Puffing pilfered Pall-Malls, sipping
swiped samples of crème de menthe,
we dreamed of escape on the battered bicycles
and oil-bleeding motorbikes
we rode in those closed-off fields,
twisting in the air like hooked trout.

I was cruising a little white Honda,
blue exhaust a smoke signal of hope,
when I spied my sixties at last.
Perched high in a sycamore,

they waved to me, forming the leaves
into the familiar, welcoming shape
of a foreign nation's friendly flag.
All my papers were signed, stamped
and sealed, rustling in a pocket
that nestled my heart.
Shifting the bike into third, its highest gear,
I waved with my left hand, palm
closest to my pulsing desire,
telling my sixties I'd soon be there.
Then, with my right, the hand
of strength, I twisted the throttle
as far as it went, then farther,
until the engine sang a new song,
the music strange but welcoming too,
and we shifted into fourth gear, then fifth
and even unto sixth.

Sawdust

The drill press could chew through a finger.
The table saw would slice off a hand.
Mr. G., before the spinning lathe,
always wore a bowtie
to keep his neck in place.

Sandpaper, far safer, was sorted by grades,
not the seventh or eighth, as we boys were,
but the coarse, the fine and the very fine.
Fine, even, as the golden hairs
on Maggie Keegan's lip.

Sawdust drifted in the air
like a fleet of tiny yachts.
They cruised a sunbeam current,
made land on our rolled-up sleeves,
and disembarked on the fine hairs
of our arms, perfuming us
with maple and pine.

O how the girls in Math would swoon
at the bold red hearts we'd made,
and all since the morning bell.

Code Name Sandalwood

Behind my bedroom door, carefully closed,
the cardboard match hissed on the first try,
then sparked on the second. As flame
passed to flame, the sandy stalk of incense
glowed red at its tip, exhaling
a velvet plume of smoke.

The box said *sandalwood*,
the letters glossy and gold
above a blue-skinned boy playing the flute,
sitting cross-legged on an emerald lawn.

I was twelve.
I'd worn sandals; I'd touched wood.
But to inhale them as one
was something new from the larger world.
The incense had come from a headshop, its air
hazy with sweet sandalwood smoke.
From behind the counter, the clerk had nodded,
black hair tapping the shoulders of his paisley vest,
smiling at the mission we were about to share.

Beatles vs. Stones

Good boys   bad boys
        we just had to choose
the sweet lick of harmony
        or the sour rasp of a lonely cry
either love   love me do
        or paint it black   devil
her turn
        to be under my thumb.

Hoping to live on the A side
        where the hits kept happening
and living a lifetime
        took 3 minutes
22 seconds

we settled instead for a day
        sometimes good
often bad
        first country
then blues
        a cockeyed music
bubbling from our lips
        the upper and the lower
the holy one
        and the sinner.

Personality Posters

Those famous faces
papering my bedroom wall
were so much more thrilling
than my mother and father's, my teachers'
dull dutiful eyes, stern and stolid mouths.

Raquel Welch, one thousand years B.C.,
barely wore a bearskin bikini,
long tanned legs
astride my inexperienced desk,

while Bela Lugosi as Dracula
scowled and skulked above the bed,
looking for virgin blood.

Mugging with a giant hookah,
the Marx Brothers confirmed my guess
that the seemingly solid adult world
shook on a scaffold of guff.

With my own face famous
merely in classroom portraits,
birthday-party Polaroids,
I could hardly wait for the day or night
when I'd flower with colors bold enough—
passionate red, expert blue—
to merit a personality poster of my own
in deepest black and white.

Motown Moves

The fury of Motown soul
and its yearning fire,
I didn't know
until Lorraine, Marcella and Denise
brought their 45s to school.
I'd never before seen anyone
palm a stack of glistening discs,
then poke long-nailed thumbs through the holes
like a turntable's silver spindle,
just as I'd never before heard
laughing and crying in a single note.

As the classroom bell rang,
Lorraine, Marcella and Denise
played a pink plastic record player in the hall.
Dancing the Funky Chicken,
their slender brown arms formed angles
my sixth-grade geometry couldn't compute.
With the Tighten Up, the Pony,
their narrow hips swung moves
I hadn't seen in gym.

Names I'd heard whispered on the wind—
Stevie Wonder, Smokey Robinson,
ladies and gentlemen, Diana Ross
and the Supremes—now beckoned me
with the reluctant arms of a nation
torn in two. They promised a trip
down into the Earth's molten core,
then a lift straight up to heaven.

Hearing those songs overflow
with a grapevine's suspicion,
with sweat running cold, and so much love,
it must be stopped
in the name of a battered heart,

my ears were lifted
as if by an ocean swell.

Two towns over,
shards of shopfront windows
paved the streets with frustration and rage.
Lorraine, Marcella and Denise
danced with their eyes closed,
dreaming, I guessed, of better times,
their feet moving lightly,
as if over crushed glass.
I watched them for a nod, a look, a sign
of what to do, how to reach across,
but they were too far away,
and I did not know
how to move in close.

Suzy Creamcheese

was what we called her
    snickering behind her back
as if we were clever

as if we understood
how urgent our longing
    to drown
in the satin quicksand of her skin
to disappear slowly
    within the parted mystery of her smile
to become forever lost
    in the labyrinth of her caramel hair

as if we knew how girl
    turning woman
was everything our hearts throbbed for
all our lungs hoped to inhale

and as if earning a cheap laugh
    would fill our shopping cart of love
we gave her a name from a song
we also didn't understand

Hitchhiking for Beginners

First, don't hitch at all.
Just grunt a goodbye,
slam the front door
for emphasis. Then take a hike.
Stand like a statue on the roadside,
impervious to the wind.
Smile into traffic
as though you were Houdini
and your next trick required
only a passing Ford.

Raise the arm that hugs the road
in the worshipful emulation of a migrating dove.
Then point your thumb in the direction
of your dearest dream.

Give the highway its due.
Let guttered glass, green and sharp,
glisten brighter than any northern star,
the tangle of Big Red wrappers,
tiny accordions of Camel butts
reveal themselves for what they are:
encrypted invitations to life,
to which you now hold the key.

Let long hair be your visa
honored in rusting vans, roach-smoking Beetles.
Notice how the wind
blasting through a rolled-down window
feels better than any other wind,
and how the sun, glittering
through a cracked windshield,
outshines every sun back home.

To travel like this is to fly
free and high, like a kettle of kites.

Staying home, you'd only sigh,
hunting for clouds in a bathroom stain.

Ahead, let the road stretch a thousand miles.
Behind, leave all but what you'd care to carry.
In between, let the promise of freedom
twist like a dancer on your outstretched thumb,
lifting your hand, turning arm to wing.

Wouldn't Have No Luck at All

Despite the lonely hours I'd invested,
the calloused tips
   my fingers had accrued,
six steel strings
   times twelve frets
weren't adding up.

Where Clapton's Strat
   had snarled and barked,
my clapped-out axe
   merely whimpered, buzzed and groaned.
Wrestling his "Crossroads"
   had me down for the count;
a barely bent B string
   pinned fingers to the mat.

So if I danced instead
to "Born Under a Bad Sign"
played even louder
   than Krakatoa
while decked out in my coolest torn T-shirt,
   dirtiest patched jeans—

Who's to say I never flew
   this close
to a star?

Greetings from Asbury Park

Hell, yeah, Bruce was one of us. Well,
best friend of a friend's older brother.
He knew the same boardwalk bars we knew,
inhaled the same sour beer, same burger fumes,
haunted the same midnight diners,
his pores oozing (like ours) with dirty coffee grinds.
His sandy lips were also cooled
by vanilla frozen custard along the seaside
and puffs of perfect Marlboro rings
forming haloes above the boardwalk's beams.

But no, Bruce wasn't like us at all.
The night in the high school gymnasium,
he took the stage like a winged god
making a late-night emergency call.
Jangling his beat-up Telecaster
the way November shakes a tree
until the leaves feel grateful for the chance to fall,
he spat out our dreams in full formation.
The drums pulsed a backbeat from our perspiration;
the keyboards convulsed with our secret rhymes.

Then we loved him
for everything he wasn't,
not our small-town despair,
nor our adolescent ennui,
not even our indolence,
which we'd ride like a sleeper car
rattling through the night.

Later, he was carried in limousines,
the windows tinted, nearly black,
a giant rearview mirror
providing the only view.
When he looked for us there,
he saw his own shadow
and the outlines of boys
we used to be.

II

Time does not take time off.
—*Augustine*

Dialing the Muse

Muse, pick up. I need your help.
Your voicemail, overflowing,
won't admit my single cry.
The hundred emails I sent you
all bounced back,
unopened, unread, seemingly
unloved. My texts to you disappear
into the ether, which is where
I'd expect you to dwell.

Maybe it's true
the spirit lives forever.
But my aging flesh
won't rattle this way again.
So never mind bringing me fish tacos,
avocado toast or ice-cold brew.
Just breathe into my keyboard.
Inspire me. Excite me. Help me
break through.

Do you demand a sacrifice?
Then take this sheet from a murdered tree,
scribbled on with squid-black ink.
I'll even mail it in an old-fashioned envelope—
relic of Mercury, the messenger god—adorned
with a tacky postage stamp
bearing the face of the singer
who died the way you like them—
young.

The perky teenaged poet,
the twenty-something playwright,
the preternaturally pert twelve-year-old
typing fan fiction from her bed—
their calls, I'm told, you answer
and on the very first ring.
Congress gives breaks to billionaires,
who don't need them.
Come on, muse. I do.

All Dressed in Green

In the latest issue of *Quagmire*
I find seven new poems by Billy Collins.
In the new *Kiss My Quarterly,*
12 poems by Billy Collins.
Coming soon in *Broken Meter*, 18 poems
by Billy Collins. On NPR radio, Billy Collins reads
"Wish I'd Written That." In my sleep,
Billy Collins stars in a major motion picture
directed by Billy Collins, produced by Billy Collins
and featuring a supporting cast
of thousands of Billy Collinses.

Tonight, at my local Barnes & Starbucks,
Billy Collins is giving a reading,
so naturally I go, all dressed in green,
color of envy, money and snot.
Other striving poets fill nearly every seat,
each wearing something green,
each moving their lips as they quietly pray,
"O gods of poetry, whoever you are,
please let a magic morsel fly
from the mouth of Billy Collins
and infect me, like a virus,
with whatever he has: The virus
of being published,
the virus of selling books,
the virus of success."

I sneer at them: "Stupid poets,"
I think, "That's not how life works."
But when Billy Collins appears at last,
smiling and nodding, clearing his throat,
I find my seat in the very front row,
open my mouth as wide as it goes,
and breathe.

To Unquenchable Ambition

Now that you gust again,
my sails are full,
both the stolid mainsail
and adventurous jib.
I wonder why I let myself
believe your powers are mine.
Without you, I'd flap uselessly,
luff, linger and flail.

Now how many sins
have I committed in your name?
At midnight, they march before me.
Here I am, groveling
for a nonentity's approval.
And here, accepting a shameful task
that should have cracked my skull.
Now I'm laughing at some lame joke
told by a mediocrity
I hoped would favor our cause.
I'd repent, but who'd forgive me?
You're the only god I know.

In the morning,
I sanitize our work with pretty names:
Getting ahead.
    Making a dent.
        Leaving something behind.
Words written in sand with a splintered stick
just before the flood tide swells.

Last night I swore
I'd ghost along without you.
Yet this morning, when your blasts resumed,
again I hoisted sail, this time
even the spinnaker,
beginner's green and peacock blue.

Filled with your foul, pestilential breath,
they swelled like carcasses rotting in the sun.
And I, instead of being sickened by the stench,
I swelled, too, with a foolish pride,
as if I'd imported at great cost and trouble
a delicious perfume, both precious and rare.

Late Bloomer

Dark gardener, take your pick:
Russian sage, purple phlox
or Turtlehead. But please,
when you come to my row,
pass by; don't pluck me yet.

All roads lead to fall,
season of the harvest mind.
But my tardy fruit sprouts
from a stubborn seed
that's snailishly slow to grow.

How I envy the apple
that blushes in May.
My slow-mo buds
merely mosey, feeble
as February's sun.

Give me one more try.
My burden has been heavy,
also great. Let this still-green stalk
flower. Persistent as you are,
what's a thirty-year wait?

Boardwalk Blues

Here, where cones of frozen custard
once thrilled,
and nostril-curling cups of fries
dripped melted curds of day-glo cheese,
I heard the sand sing songs of change,
and the wind was humming along.

Now the boardwalk's dusty timbers
splinter and split, spit rusty nails.
Even the fortune teller's booth,
boarded up and empty,
keeps a secret of the past.

The wind still blows
but the sand seems tired,
so much disappointed dirt
that once upon a time was stone.

How I'd like to shake their hands,
I who also hoped to change the world
with nothing more than air.

Crass Beauty

When our English teacher quipped, "Mr. Krass,
        please don't be so crass,"
I, teenaged ass, didn't even know the word.

The dictionary quickly cut me down:
        1) gross, 2) unrefined, 3) crude.
Our family name, my dented sword.

We couldn't hail back to Marcus Crassus,
        ignoble robber of Rome,
for our lineage was shorter by far,

just two generations, when Grandpa Krasnitsky
        deflated our name, his English
mostly broken, chronically crippled, hit and missed.

Krassy-assy, the mean kids called me.
        And I, lacking a sassy comeback,
cursed my luck until I learned

Kras- in Slavic meant beauty and red.
        Krasny Oktyabr hums a candy box,
delicious gift from a far-flung friend.

That's *Red October*, start of several ends,
        and beauty on beauty, for as Ovid notes,
October out-beauties all other months.

Even now my crassitude weighs on me, especially
        in pajamas. That's where I dream
of Krasnodar, Krasnoyarsk and even Krasnopolyansky,

Russian red cities of indescribable beauty.
        Indescribable because I've never seen them.
Beautiful and red for that reason too.

Grandpa's ignorance wasn't my bliss.
   More like a crevasse in the language,
a hole that threatened to swallow me whole. Is that crass?

Still a Krass can dream
       of strolling Krasny Prospekt, bathing
in the multitude, oozing nothing but crassness

from his knee-high boots to his Astrakhan hat.
   "What that remarkable man?" a visitor wonders.
"Oh, him," a helpful local replies. "That's our Mr. Beauty."

Hoboken

At 3 a.m. my dead friends visit me.
The bars closed, they scrounge around
for Swiss fondue, bananas and costly cigars.
Limping on bad legs, they wear boaters and bow ties,
pull their hair back into a ponytail,
wax their moustaches like villains in old cartoons.

Though my friends mean to guide me
through my difficulties, they strangely insist
two plus two could equal five,
that is, if you really want it to. Che Guevara
was the prime minister of Afghanistan.
Hoboken is the secret capital of Brazil.

Somehow I know it's just a movie,
and I love old movies, so I smile in my sleep
as the images of my dead friends
roll across my eyelids.
They're like slides projected on a screen
my father used to unfold after family vacations.

Then, in our darkened living room,
Saddleback Mountain would tower overhead, the air
scented with birch bark and fern, hawks
screeching in the crisp, cold air. "This,"
my father would say, "is another view from the chairlift."
Laughing, my brothers and I would call out for more,
until at last came the final slide, a picture of a lonely tree
clinging to gravel and juniper moss.
The show over, we'd yawn, then blink our eyes
at the sudden light, as if waking from a dream
so pleasant, so reassuring,
it almost could come true.

Fatherhood

In a world made of water
my father was seltzer—
good to have around
    when the house caught on fire.

His reputation flowed with the tides
both the flood's enlivening swirl and churn
and the ebb's reversal, sailing
    drowned leaves and dead dragonflies
far out to sea.

Now I am a father too.
Like my father
I celebrate Independence Day
   as if I knew how it feels.

In books I read how life
   first pulsed at sea
how bubbles and buoyant foam
   fathered flecked tentacles
     fingery fins
then at last two bold feet
   to dominate even rock.

The rain knocks on my door.
I don't answer.

I stand on pure rock
   craving the pucker of seawater
     the burnt sand in my shoes
both the shoes I can fill
and the ones I never will.

Outsourcing My Grief

Five years after my father's death,
I've discovered a Chinese factory
where you can outsource your grief.
Built on the edge of a giant city
whose name I'd never heard,
the factory has six thousand workers.
Early each morning, they practice tai chi,
easing the sun's components
into the supply chain of the dawn.

Now, for just $19 a month,
the workers mourn on my behalf,
performing graceful lotus kicks
that raise my father's spirit
like a kite, then send it soaring
high into a forgetful cloud.

So pleased am I with the results,
I've upgraded. Now, in addition,
a troupe of the factory's best workers
recall with traditional song and dance
the fading instance of my father's death.
At the end, they raise overhead
a small white stone
for exactly thirty seconds, the time it took
for my father's heart to stop.

It seems to be working.
I laugh again. I can read the morning news
and without wiping my eyes.
Still, I worry: What if every American did this?
Wouldn't our side of the planet
lighten with a forgetful ease
while China's side became bloated,
swollen by the mass of our outsourced grief?
I asked the factory foreman about it.

"Don't worry," he replied.
"We're used to the grief.
So is the Earth."

Twice a year, the factory sends me
my father's status report.
The latest update says his spirit
floats halfway between heaven
and earth, weightless
as a hungry ghost, munching on tofu,
chicken feet and rice. They say
his spirit sings, as it rarely did in life:
Thank you, everyone, thank you.
Thank you very, very much.

The Weather Man

Roger, when I finally snap and you find me
raving like a madman in the frozen street,
remember, it's better this way, I'm happier,
now that I no longer have to pretend.

Think of all the years I had to act
as if I cared about recycling, saving for that rainy day,
how many calories I could save by eating kale,
or what that client really thought about my work.

The weather inside and the weather outside
never matched, forming a pressure zone so high,
it could crack the Brooklyn Bridge in two.

So when they cry and say it's a shame, set them straight.
Tell them the sun finally shines on both my sides,
and the rain—oh, how lovely when the rain comes pouring in.

Old Dog

Older than dirt and three times as tired,
I'm winded by the distance
from one day to the next.
Until now I never knew
how warm an inch of hair could be,
or how Fortune and Luck,
that grizzled pair of bitches,
laugh at me late at night.

A TV channel I've never heard of
cancels a series I never watched.
One friend moves tentatively
out to the country.
Another friend moves permanently
into the past.

The old dog remains,
sitting faithfully at my feet.
Gazing up my way with chocolate eyes,
she sees a world
she too can't understand.

My Sixties

Sometimes, to keep me lively,
my sixties insist on showing me
the distant bank of that shaded strait
no swimmer can cross but once.
That's when they also make me feel
those chilly gusts of fetid air
that, filled with their own emptiness,
haunt the black water's ripples like a ghost.
Then too they toss alongside my feet
a heavy pile of freshly turned earth
taken from that dank, damned place
where time does not take time off.

Awakened, I feel them scramble my thoughts
with the toast and broken eggs.
When my name rings out on the kitchen tiles,
I look around for a stranger.
My face stares back from the spoon's concave,
resembling no one I've ever known.

Other days my sixties encourage me
with favorable portents, hopeful signs.
In the hospital waiting room (a frightened field
of anxious faces), the night nurse smiles,
"Couldn't tomorrow be that beautiful day?"

Sometimes, late at night, my sixties show me
old movies, grainy dreams in black and white
saturated with remembrance, regret and rue.
In one I play the heartless villain
who twirls a curled waxed moustache
while tying his sweetheart to the tracks
where no train has run for at least seven years.
In another, I'm the earnest young fool
who sacrifices all to a vengeful god
he no longer believes exists.

I like my sixties best when they show me
a chilled glass of flaxen beer
spilling over with gratitude,
its foam afire with effervescent hope.
Or how an old book, precious gift
from a long-departed friend,
speaks to me in his unforgotten voice.

And the dark sky's crescent moon!
Only now can I see how its twin tips
pierce the night's black cape
like the bloodied horns of a bull.
Panting alone in the stilled arena,
he stamps one still-mighty leg
and silently gasps:
"Nearly beaten, yes;
almost vanquished, of course;
practically a memory, true;
but all of these not yet, not yet—
no, I tell you, not yet."

PJ Krass grew up in central New Jersey and now lives in Brooklyn, N.Y. His poems have appeared in journals including *Adirondack Review*, *Atlanta Review*, *Chaleur*, *New Verse News*, *South Carolina Review* and *Rattle*. He's the recipient of a Pushcart Prize Special Mention. A journalist for over two decades—with *BusinessWeek* and *Inc.*, among many other publications—PJ now works as a freelance writer and editor for clients that include *The Economist*, *Harvard Business Review*, MIT and Intel. He also teaches at The Writers Studio, and he's the poetry co-editor of an anthology, *The Writers Studio at 30*. *My Sixties* is his first chapbook.

www.ingramcontent.com/pod-product-compliance
Lightning Source LLC
LaVergne TN
LVHW041602070426
835507LV00011B/1262